American Compass

American Compass

BILL MEISSNER

University of Notre Dame Press

Notre Dame, Indiana

Manufactured in the United States of America

Library of Congress Cataloging-in-Publication Data
Meissner, William, 1948–
    American compass / Bill Meissner.
        p.   cm.
    Includes bibliographical references and index.
    ISBN 0-268-03481-8 (alk. paper)
    ISBN 0-268-03482-6 (pbk. : alk. paper)
    I. Title.
    PS3563.E38A47   2004
    811'.54—dc22
                                    2004017585

∞ *This book is printed on acid-free paper.*

For Christine and Nathan,

who help me find my way

_____

_____

_____

Also for my mother, Julie Meissner, for her encouragement,

and in memory of my father, Leonard Meissner,

who followed his dashboard compass.

contents

acknowledgments

I would like to express my gratitude to the Loft-McKnight Foundation for a Loft-McKnight Award in Poetry, the Minnesota State Arts Board for a Fellowship in Poetry, and the National Endowment for the Arts for a Poetry Fellowship.

Thanks also to Jack Driscoll for his continued support of my writing.

I would like to thank the following publications where these poems appeared:

Minnesota Monthly: "A Certain Length of Line," "Finding a Note to Myself: Throw Away Those Old Shoes," "Tough Luck Ballplayer in the Diamond Bluff Tavern," "Veteran Pitcher Whose Heart Was Stopped by a Line Drive to the Chest"

Three Rivers Poetry Journal: "Twisters," "The Old Men of Summer"

North American Review: "Piano Lessons at St. Lucy the Martyr Grade School," "Kiwi," "June Bugs in the Window of the Rapids Laundromat"

Only Believe: Elvis Writings (anthology, forthcoming): "The King Is Alive and Well at Your Neighborhood 7-11 Store"

Mid-American Review: "1963: Orbit of the Wiffle Ball"

Milkweed Chronicle: "Baseball With Steve Lyon"

Kansas Quarterly: "The Baseball Lover"

Northeast: "Ode to a Baseball Wound"

Atlanta Review: "Thomas Edison, Insomniac," "Coasting toward Heaven"

"Thomas Edison, Insomniac" was reprinted in *Atlanta Review*'s 10th Anniversary Anthology.

Studio One: "First Day of Summer Vacation: Muskrat on a Suburban Roadside," "Stalling in My New Car Near the High School," "Dance of the Ripples" [reprinted]

Lake Effect: "Hunting for Night Crawlers" [appeared in a different form]

View (The Loft Newsletter): "After the Tokens Run Out"

Minnesota Calls: "In Praise of the Everyday Cow"

Turnstile: "Judging Fly Balls Hit by My Father"

Aethlon: "Playing the Wind: Running for Fly Balls in Early Spring"

Thirty-Three Minnesota Poets (anthology, Nodin Press): "First Ties: My Father in the Mirror," "The Contortionist's Wife"

Minneapolis Review of Baseball: "The Ex-Baseball Star Steps Out of Retirement," "Aging Man, Searching for the Lost Baseball"

Reprints of the following: "Chalk Lines: Baseball with Steve Lyon," "The Baseball Lover"

Controlled Burn: "The Dance of the Ripples"

Clackamas Literary Review: "The Arrowhead," reprinted in *Kaleidoscope*

"The Baseball Lover" and "Twisters" are reprinted from *The Sleepwalker's Son*, by Bill Meissner, Ohio University Press, 1987.

"Piano Lessons at St. Lucy the Martyr Grade School" was reprinted on the CNN Money (New York) page on the World Wide Web.

International Poetry Review: "The Secret of the Intersection"

Elysian Fields Quarterly: "Surviving the Terrorism: Ode to a Baseball Wound," "The Old Men of Summer" [reprinted in another form]

Notre Dame Review: "1953: James Dean Walks the Streets of New York All Night," "The Ventriloquist and His Dummy"

Writing is like driving at night in the fog. You can only see as far as your headlights, but you can make the whole trip that way.

—E. L. Doctorow

PART ONE

First Corners

FIRST TIES:
THE FATHER IN THE MIRROR

Fourteen, late for church, I stood in front of the mirror, fumbling
with the new tie until my father's face surfaced behind me.
Reaching in front of my chest, he led
the red and blue silk around and
under, under and
around in some mysterious
pattern. *Nothing to a tie*, he said.

For those few seconds, his big arms were my arms—
I watched the thick fingers
working the tie, each time a little
too short or too long.

He leaned his face alongside mine,
and I smelled a sharp scent of Old Spice, heard the hiss of sighs
through his nose, like a car tire losing air,
as he focused on the broad wrinkled pillar
that would not tie.
Arms that hadn't surrounded me for years
now wrapped me like ribbons. I couldn't pull away
from the rough kiss of whiskers
against my smooth cheek.
With each attempt, his elbows swung
like rhythmic pendulums, and
for a few seconds it looked like we could have been
dancing, so I stood still.

He finally finished a crooked knot, slid it
up to my tender throat, too tight, too tight.
Just right, he said.

At that moment, I understood:
being an adult meant
you looked a little older, but you couldn't breathe.
  After my father backed away
  and disappeared, I stood by myself
  in the mirror, where all I could see
  was that knot at my throat, a soft, angled
  embrace of cloth.

THE CONTORTIONIST'S WIFE

She knows him, yet she doesn't always recognize him—
some mornings she finds him in the kitchen cupboard
flattened among the cereal boxes;
some evenings, he's folded beneath her chair
when she sits down for dinner.
Once he surprised her when he rose from the washing machine tub
like a genie, gave her three wishes
and a box of Cheer.

Some days she doesn't know if he's shaping himself
or if she's shaping him. All she knows is the way
he twists her emotions: he makes her laugh, he makes her cry.

She's not sure if it's funny that he
could be lying between the sheets of her bed without her
noticing him.
Sometimes he's closer to her than she ever imagined, like the
tub full of warm bath water she slides herself into.
Sometimes he's distant, pinpricks of stars in the night sky.
But most often he's both near and far, lifting himself
from the vase in the corner, his smile full of flowers.

Ah, she wishes she could be a contortionist, too.
She wishes she could be the one to surprise him
some morning, disguising herself as the wheat bread
popping from the toaster
or the coat rack as he reaches for his jacket.
She gazes at her stiff flesh with the brittle bones inside,
thinking if only she could slip herself around his finger
like a ring he didn't know he was wearing
for the rest of his life.

PIANO LESSONS AT ST. LUCY THE MARTYR GRADE SCHOOL

Though they were silent, the row of keys
always seemed to hiss at me
as I slipped that hard bench up close,
poised my hands above them for that first note,

then waited there for five years. Five
years I poised my hands
in that narrow room, and I
never got it right: each major a minor,
each A note an F, each clef a treble.
Between songs, I winced and stared
at the crucifix on the wall, felt the blood
in my fingers pulsing.

My piano teacher, Sister Angelica, dressed in her lines
of black and white, tapped my wrists
with a wooden pointer to keep them arched,
shook her head at all the wrong notes, wondering
what would ever become of me.
After I played an off-key chorus again and again,
she closed her eyes and her wrinkled face glowed red
as if she were in purgatory.
Her palms, lifted to the ashen tiled ceiling,
seemed to whisper *Stop. Please stop.*

Once, alone in the room, I lifted the heavy wooden top
of the piano, peered in, saw my future inside:
the wooden hammers, their dry wood splitting,
the confused black lines
of wire, all those sour notes
they'd hold too long.

Before the all-school concert, in the lavatory,
I flattened my cowlick with Brylcreem.
Deep in the mirror, a kid played a jazzy song, nimble fingers
dancing on the cool porcelain sink.

Standing off stage behind the musty curtain, listening
for my name to buzz through the tin speakers in the gym ceiling,
I squeezed the *Flowers in Spring* sheet music in my palm.
Then I crossed the stage, my back rigid,
thinking about that song I could play so perfectly
in my dreams.

I lowered myself
to the sticky enameled bench,
my shirt tucked in too tightly,
and stared at the endless keys. Like the rows of people
in the audience, they grinned at me,
just waiting for that first mistake.

JUNE BUGS IN THE WINDOW OF THE RAPIDS LAUNDROMAT

Summoned by the glowing square,
hundreds of them
thump against the pane.

June bugs can't hold to slippery glass;
they fly clumsily, thunk and thunk, then
tick on their backs on the sidewalk,
legs swimming
until a boy's bicycle tire
crackles them on cement.

Or they fly up again, as if
there's something inside they can't live without:
the brightness of light, and all those sheets folding and
unfolding their large white wings.

Inside, women's fingers crawl over pages of movie magazines.
Eyelids like husks, they've forgotten
the beauty of circling.
One of them stands,
stares through her stoic reflection.
Chevy tires spin at the stop sign.
She presses her fingertips like white dimes
on the window. She can almost see the distance
to her house, her husband waiting
in the lit window.

She leans her forehead against the pane,
her wrinkles smoothing.
A June bug flies toward her cheek,
thumps into glass.
Before it drops to the pavement it whirrs a few seconds,
as if falling in love with the pale moon of her face.

KIWI

The scent of shoe polish,
as my Dad rubbed a cloth over his wing tips in the morning,
was a rich, dark brown aroma:
a scent of paneled sales showrooms with rows and rows
of copper banks, of a pile of pennies
scooped up with the palm of a hand,
a scent of departure.

I was five, and always laughed at the small brown Kiwi bird
on the tin cover of the shoe polish. I'd never seen
that long-beaked, stick-legged bird in central Iowa.
Dad said they lived halfway
around the world, and probably were extinct.
A *bird with wings that small can't fly,* he told us.

Telephone poles anchored our small town
to the center of Iowa, the flat fields
stretching all the way to the horizon.
Invisible strings of radio waves were our only ties to the world,
and the world was commercials for Tide,
crackling grain and livestock reports from Sioux City,
gains and losses I never understood.

When my father drove us on vacation,
I stared nervously at paint-chipped white crosses
planted along the highway roadsides, each one marking
a place where someone died. I pictured their bodies,
pulled from the wreckage of cars and buried beneath the crosses,
black-eyed Susans and dandelions
sprouting from their hearts.

In the morning Dad finished polishing his shoes,
slipped on his gray felt hat, smiled, then stepped
toward his '59 Rambler. *He'll be gone five days,*
Mom whispered to us, her voice like the sheets on the clothesline,
rising, falling. *But he'll quit this job soon, soon.*
Then the house fell quiet, as if holding its breath
before a storm, as if about to surrender shutters and shingles
and roof to an onrushing twister.

Older, I realized that he never crossed the Iowa border
on those sales trips,
but back then I pictured him driving and driving
halfway around the world to a place
from which he could never return.
I heard sirens in the still Iowa night,
roadside crosses sprouted in my sleep.

Older, I understood it was a kind of love that made him leave,
a kind of love that brought him back every few days, as Mom and I
waited for hours on that sagging front porch.

When he finally pulled into the driveway,
he slid from the driver's side, stepped out stiffly
as though he'd forgotten how to walk.
His scuffed shoes brushed through the splintered grass
as I rushed toward him,
the Kiwi polish squeezed tightly in one hand,
the brown-stained cloth fluttering from the other.

THE PROMISE OF WHEATIES

Every morning I poured those misshapen flakes
into my green plastic bowl,
studied the orange box that boasted: *Breakfast of Champions*.
I splashed them with milk and ate them,
savoring the soggy brown flakes as if they were slices of gold,
and dreamed of Mickey Mantle, my skinny arms
thickening like his.
I believed. I believed the television
beneath the gleam of my father's trophies,
believed in the cardboard box and Mickey Mantle's smile,
which whispered that mornings filled with Wheaties
would make muscles curl around my bones like vines.
I dreamed of hitting a baseball so far
it would break through the ceiling of the sky.
For me, a small boy standing
in the center of my yard in the center of America,
there was no orbit too large.
For years I filled bowl after bowl of Wheaties until
the boxes emptied, one after the other, until the flimsy wax paper
crackled, the last pieces clinking
into the bowl like dropped coins.

The promise of Wheaties was so strong.
How could I know they were just cardboard words?
How could I know that, years later,
the satellites from the 1960s would, one by one, re-enter the
earth's atmosphere and burn to cinders?

On my eighteenth birthday I stood in front of the living room mirror
with my shirt off, the cloth of my pants gathering
in khaki pools at my shoe tops. I glared
at the thin arms I knew could not hit a baseball beyond my yard,
glared at my small fists, wanting to throw a punch
at my chest—that flat, bony map, that country
where I knew I was banished to live
for the rest of my life.

COASTING TOWARD HEAVEN

They finally took out the confessional at St. Joseph's church;
They've remodeled for the Lord.
Now the place where my friends and I
confessed our first real sins is gone, leaving
just a bare wall with a rectangular, shadowy stain
where the wooden booth stood for eighty years.

Back in seventh grade, we rode laboriously to the church, full to
bursting with lying and stealing and swearing and gawking
at girlie magazines in Kluge's Gas.
Each sin leaves a stain, the nuns told us, and we believed
every word. I imagined my soul as a white blotter, smudged
to the corners with gray.
We steered our bicycles carefully—
Tommy said if a car hit us before we got to the church,
we'd go straight to hell.
Think of it, Tommy:
Eighty years of sins, coloring
the dark inside of that confessional even blacker—
adult sins, much heavier than ours, weighing down
the musty air inside the booth so it took
a dozen workmen just to lift it.

After Tommy and I confessed behind the sweating curtain,
we circled the playground gracefully with no hands,
gambled at intersections, and coasted full speed
down the cracked sidewalk of Hospital Hill
to our houses, where our mothers asked us
where we'd been and we answered "Nowhere."
We'd eat dinners silently, then go to our rooms
where we'd lie on our beds,
our minds clear for one day, our bodies
    feeling so light we thought we were floating above the mattress
    as we drifted toward that pure, dark sleep.

STALLING IN MY NEW CAR NEAR
THE HIGH SCHOOL

Four years were streamers of crepe paper, fluttering,
then dissolving in the murky river.

You remember the girls tapping pencils between their legs
on desk chairs, boys rubbing
thumbs across erasers.

You remember blackboards
filled with chalky equations:
weekends, you wiped them clean
with beer-stained sleeves.
Girlfriends, cashmere sweaters soft as foam, lied to you
behind the woolen mills,
whispering of rowboats and eternity.

At the end of senior year, you ran into the parking lot,
your laughter joyous as the dirt devils
spiraling above the gravel.
A few days after graduation, some of your friends grabbed guns,
some anchored themselves to desks, some just
lay down on the center line of the county highway
as though they needed a rest.

Older, you see your former teachers downtown, trudging
beneath the town clock that's eight hours behind.
They no longer recognize your face—to them, you're just
another adult, your face creased
like the paper airplanes you tossed across the classroom
whenever their back was turned.

Four years are spray paint on a cement wall
the rain washed off.

You still drive by it now and then—
that old building, that smudged front window
you always wanted to break,
that window now too opaque to see in.

THE SECRET OF THE INTERSECTION

"Listen," he whispers.
Leaning close to him in the hospital bed,
  I taste the dust he must have tasted
  for thirty years on all those county roads, dust
  that settled on the shoulders of his white shirt
  as his '59 Rambler traced a path across the broad back of Iowa.
The white lines sliding beneath his car were dashes
  in the Morse code of traveling salesmen,
  and he understood every word.
Inside the compass mounted on the dash, the needle, bobbing
  in the liquid, always knew where to go.

I lean toward him, seeing, behind his eyes,
  the blue buzzing neon inside café windows,
  shiny stacks of washing machine brochures,
  mute maps folded so often they tore, the waterfall
  of silver dropping into pay phones.
"Soon, soon," he'd tell Mom. He'd buy paint
  for the peeling gray pillars that held up our
  porch, pink pillowcases to buoy up our dreams.

Back then, the world was flat:
  at unmarked intersections,
  he'd stop and pile a pyramid of gravel
  on the roadside so he'd find his way back.
He could never have guessed that, one day,
  the dashboard compass would fail him,
  all the liquid evaporated from it.

I lean closer. I believe, after all these years,
he'll tell me the secret of the intersection.
"Listen."

I strain to hear his words, expecting them to glide
steadily from his throat: freight cars
on polished tracks, porcelain coffee cups across Formica.
Like a person going deaf,
I lean too close to his face,
the skin of my ear brushing his creased lips.

And that's when I hear it:
his eyes roll upward slowly, an odometer turning over,
and he exhales a long rasping sigh,
a sigh that must say everything he needed to say—
    a sudden gust of wind filling a backyard,
    lifting a clean white shirt
    on a clothesline, then
    letting it fall again.

PART TWO

Braking Dreams

THOMAS EDISON, INSOMNIAC

How could you dream so much
when you slept so little?
How could you, pacing the floor of your lab,
imagine light, unfolding like some bright flower
caught inside a glass bulb?

Necessity, they say. And you searched,
your brain twisted like a spiraling filament through the endless
labyrinth, toward
a narrow pinhole of light,
so you alone could see.

Those long hours at night, you needed something
to illuminate the room besides the blood in your brain
turning incandescent.
You needed a future, and it was out there somewhere,
illusive as static just before lightning.

Oh, America was waiting for you, Thomas. There would be
headlights on cars and 3-D movies and searchlights at Wal-Mart,
there would be ultraviolet and lasers and night vision for wars,

but you knew none of this. You stood
for hours in your wrinkled pajamas,
in a room with one fluttering candle,
unable to sleep, thinking how much you hated
the endless blackness
that pressed itself against the paned window each night.

Necessity, they say. Look, Thomas, you finally
found what you needed: a bright globe on your desk.
It was enough for you,
for everyone—something small and shining
to comfort the lonely who pace and pace for hours
in the deepest vacuum of night.

THE VENTRILOQUIST
AND HIS DUMMY

Making sure your lips are asleep is what the mirror taught you.
Behind your tight smile, you learned
to pronounce each word
as though it were fine glass.

As a child you were too shy
for words. You pocketed them
in a cloth bag like marbles.
So you've spent a lifetime trying to will wood
out of its ancient silence,
learned to throw your voice
to the farthest corners,
his red enameled grin waiting to catch it.
You try your best to make the audience laugh, or sob,
to feel the knots in their stomachs.

Sometimes, propping the dummy on your knee,
you catch yourself thinking
you should trim his fingernails, offer him a glass of milk.
Other times, when the hinges on his jaw stutter,
you think of pounding his hardwood head
on the stage floor, his brain
smashed to splinters.

After the show, you're too deeply asleep to hear
his raspy throat inside the latched suitcase
repeating, one by one,
all the words
you really needed to say.

1953: JAMES DEAN WALKS THE STREETS OF NEW YORK ALL NIGHT

All your life you walked in the middle of the street.
The night buries your hands in your pockets,
wrinkles your clothes like the folds in your brain
where you search and search, but can't find
sleep.

You don't know the reason you walk,
but it's something about America.
It's about the theater marquee lightbulbs above you
that have darkened and cooled, it's about
the damp matches in your pocket and the fuse
to the atomic bomb. It's about the silence of this
night that won't stop exploding in your ear.

You could be the only
person alive in New York after the fallout.
There are no answers, man; just a few good questions.
You taught us that.
Some nights there's no shelter, no warning siren. There's only
that huge sky above that keeps tossing its useless coins,
there's only the sheen of the abandoned
street stretching endlessly in front of you.

In time, the rain stops, but the dreams keep breaking.
They break with each
step, ring out in circles like shock waves, then vanish
at the edge
of the black and silver puddles.

IN PRAISE OF THE EVERYDAY COW

1

Look: Holstein cows in a field, all pointing toward the same direction
like huge black and white compasses!
They lead us to the true north of green grass.
It's amazing how a cow can stay in small pastures all day,
content, as if reading the horizon like an endless book,
as if the three most important things in the world are
chewing, and staring,
and chewing.

2

I confess that, as a reckless youth, I have sneaked into
pastures under cover of darkness.
I have witnessed, in the middle of the night,
the ancient ritual of cow-tipping.
I have watched vandals push a sleeping cow from its standing position
onto its side, where it kicked its legs for a moment
as if it were dreaming of flying.

3

Have you ever looked closely into a cow's eyes?
The beauty of a cow is that it's hard to tell whether it's awake
or asleep. Those deep, liquid eyes just stare back at you
and beyond you with a kind of indifferent love.
Acceptance. That's the cow's motto.
It doesn't matter if you're black
with white spots, or white with black spots—it's all the same.

4

I have a cure for our hungry, overcrowded planet:
Let us all have pet cows.
Let us keep them in our backyards and, each night,
lead them to the porch or basement so there'll be no more tipping.
Let us pat them on their broad, flat foreheads
where their fur swirls in concentric patterns like galaxies.

Let us have enough milk for the whole world to drink.

JOE DIMAGGIO'S THIRST

Every day for hours you charged grounders in the outfield
so your fielding would be smooth, a liquid
spilled from a glass on a bright green
countertop. You ran full speed, Joe,
scooped up America in your glove,
and all in one motion you threw her home.

Marilyn's arms were waiting there, behind home plate.
Your throw was taut and perfect, clipping
the blades of infield grass as it bounced
true. In '41 your arm could have cut
down Hitler trying to score from third.

In '49 you batted .357 and circled the base paths,
racing through the dusty ghosts
of Ruth and Gehrig.
You drove the baseballs hard, and
the Yankee sky, a bright blue mouth,
opened for each hit. The whole country opened its mouth
for you, Joe; Marilyn parted her lips, turning the sky
sunset pink, and we all said *Ahhhh*.

Ah, Joe. How
could we know that, all in one
motion, you'd wave your blue cap and retire, all
in one motion, you and Marilyn would part, and
the years would part for you in silence, each one
huge and quiet
as an empty stadium at night?

How could we know you'd surface, decades later,
as Mr. Coffee on the TV screen, your big hand wrapped
around a plastic cup, your arm gone
stiff, your hair
washed uniform gray?

After the commercial, you
sat alone at the dull green table,
your head bowed.
Though you didn't notice, the sleeve of your suit jacket
soaked up your spilled coffee
as if it were dying of thirst.

ODE TO THE CHEVY NOVAS, 1962–1979:
A SIX CYLINDER CONCERTO WITH
MUFFLER ACCOMPANIMENT

1

It doesn't matter that they rust and rust until you can't tell what color they are. Doesn't matter that their bald tires hold their breaths, their mufflers drag down the street, sparks flying behind like meteors. What matters is they run, they run. What matters is the owners love them, jack up their back ends so the cars always roll down hill. And though the car's only going the limit, inside, it feels like you're traveling at the speed of light.

2

Owners pamper their Novas in driveways, their hoods lifted toward the sky as if in prayer. They decorate the plastic dashboards with a silvery frosting of losing lottery tickets. On cold winter mornings, before they try to coax the carburetors to consciousness, the drivers bear precious gifts of offering to hang on rearview mirrors: graduation tassels, air fresheners shaped like keys, black lace wedding-night garters, fuzzy dice.

3

In Spanish, the words "No va" mean "Does not go."
The model did not sell particularly well in Mexico.

4

My '72 Nova survived a tree falling on it. After a tornado knocked a huge elm across the driveway, the amazed city crew, sawing the limbs, found the car intact—its finish smiling dully, the only damage a few small dents in the roof. At dusk, inside the car, I reached up with the palm of my hand, and, like a lover or a blind man, I tenderly popped out the dents.

5

Loyal Nova owners never sell their cars, even when the engines go comatose. They simply tow them out back with the other Novas lined up like oversized lawn ornaments, and gaze out at them as they eat supper. Late at night, from upstairs windows, owners sometimes think they see the headlights flare.

6

But some Novas eventually end up compacted into those rectangles you see in salvage yards. Though the car's been crushed, the owners are sure that, just as easy as gasoline evaporates, its spirit has gone to a better place. In the Heaven of Novas, it enjoys its rewards: endless straightaways of smooth asphalt, AM radios that play static-free, odometers that reverse themselves to zero, and mufflers, oh mufflers that no longer rust out every six months.

THE KING IS ALIVE AND WELL AT
YOUR NEIGHBORHOOD 7-11 STORE

Elvis, we couldn't let you go out like that,
so we brought you back for an encore
at our local convenience store.
We see you there at 2 a.m., puffy face hidden
from the fluorescent lights
beneath the huge black wings
of your sunglasses, stirring your coffee with a slight
sway of your hips. We see you slipping last week's *Enquirer*
under your black jacket, lifting
a box of Fudgsicles for your late snack.

Elvis, we can't decide if it's funny or not
that we still see you everywhere we go,
that we still hear your voice, exhaling
the ordinary air like music.
We can't decide whether to laugh or cry. So instead
we just stare, Elvis, at what we want you to be:
we see you in Vegas, your sequined shirt flashing
as you rush to a limo.
We see you at a shelter in Memphis, the scarf around
your neck a tattered white noose,
your upper lip quivering over a bowl of soup.
Some see you middle aged, in a business suit. They're certain
you're on your way to heaven as you
drive a Cadillac across Tennessee forever.

Still others simply see you as the leather-jacketed kid
playing pinball in the corner of the 7-11.
Anxious for replays, he urges the score with his thighs until
the machine tilts, and though he keeps
snapping the buttons, the silver ball
whirrs across the table beneath
darkened glass, disappears
between the motionless
flippers.

THE MAN WHO WRESTLED
THE LAWN

There's always a weed here, a weed there, poking
their sharp noses through his dreams.
Everywhere he looks, there's too much crabgrass,
too little sunlight, never enough chance
of rain. He marches into his yard;
the vinyl snake of the hose coils around his leg
and he's Ahab, drowning
in the unkempt green sea.

At hardware stores, he catches himself gazing longingly
at stocky Briggs and Stratton mowers, browsing aisles
of power leaf blowers, hedge trimmers, yard edgers, weed whackers
that could cut the knees off a whole army of green.
He never rests from this endless mowing and digging and trimming,
this edging and raking and mulching.
His wife and children watch from
afar, flowers in pots he tends to once a week.
His friends are dried wreaths kept in the attic.
His life is dedicated to battle, his mission
to cut the chaos, to poison the thistled opposition
before it flaps its prickly lime tongue.
A *weed is death*, he thinks, *and death is a weed*.
His mornings are an extra-sturdy plastic ground cloth unrolling,
clean wood chips covering it all the way to the horizon.
His afternoon is spigots and sprinklers,
double-thick white cloth gloves gripping the neck
of a Garden Weasel 'til it chokes. Dusk
is a gray Lawn Boy moving in from the east, its thick wheels
spinning at the flip of a switch.
By June, he'll have the best yard in the neighborhood,
his row of *Ace* rakes standing at attention in the garage.

After he's in his grave,
a groundskeeper on a riding lawn mower might pause above him.
Somehow, from deep under the soil, he'll feel the mower's vibrations,
its humming, humming,
soothing him to sleep.
His face, polished as a decorative stone,
will look serene, finally, perfect
as an overcast morning sky with a sure promise of rain.

JAMES DEAN, RESURRECTED

After the crash, after the last long song of the tires
and the sudden crescendo of metal
on metal, you open your eyes
and look beyond the mapped windshield:
the California desert has become
your boyhood farm in Indiana
where you used to swing across
the barn rafters, riding the air, holding tight
to a fraying rope.
   Below, cows turn their soft, slow
   faces toward you, unimpressed.
   "Look," you want to say as you watch
   yourself glide again through shafts of grainy light, "That was me."

Somehow you lift your whole body slowly
and you rise from the embrace of the dashboard.
Though the radio has gone silent,
the anthem of a new country plays in your ear.
You cross the center line to the eastbound lane and watch
as the wreckage hisses, the red antifreeze pools
on the asphalt while an ambulance rescue team tries
to revive some boy caught in a cage of chrome.
Stupid American kid—
he had nowhere to go, and he just had to get there
fast.

You shake your head and grin your wry grin,
turn your collar up, and lean
toward the smooth asphalt, taking your time,
sticking out your thumb to hitch a ride.

PART THREE

_____

_____

_____

Taking the Curve

CHALK LINES: BASEBALL
WITH STEVE LYON

Steve and I could see chalk lines all the way to the majors.

For us, any long patch of grass
was a roaring stadium.
Day after day it was pitch, hit, field:
run for weeks to catch a long fly. Dive
for the tough fast ones just out of
reach, come up tasting
dust and grass stains and white leather.

By mid-season, the two of us were a whole team.

    (How could we know that ten years later
    we'd end up swinging shovels in factories,
    pitching waste baskets, squeezing
    slow beers in bars, ignoring
    the blaring ball game on the TV?)

Near the end of summer before freshman year,
we sat winded on tin folding chairs at Kluge's Gas,
oceans of sweat gone from the bills of our caps.
We sipped strawberry sodas and stared
straight ahead beyond paint chips on the wall,
thinking only of the beautiful line drives of our futures.

JUDGING FLY BALLS HIT BY MY FATHER

The afternoon he lost his job, he dragged the wooden bat
through the heavy air
and hit fly balls to me.
Still wearing his shiny black salesman's shoes,
his legs stiff from the long drive,
he poised in the powdered dirt near the plate,
paunchy in his shirt that glowed like a white flag,
the baseball in his hand bald as he'd be in a few years.

He hit me fly ball after fly ball,
grunting each time he swung.
His red and blue tie, knotted in the wires of the backstop,
flapped its dry tongue.
The scuffed ball drew looping lines in the air, always
just beyond my glove.
I was just a kid; it was hard for me
to judge where they'd fall.

Later he hit some long ones.
"Don't try to catch these," he told me.
Crouched behind the small snow fence in center,
I watched, my fingers curled in the rough wood slats.
He hit one that rose until I thought it would scrape the sun.
When it began to fall right toward me,
I squeezed a splinter into my thumb.
But the ball died up there, pushed back by the breeze
gusting in from center. It
landed harmlessly in front of the fence,
losing itself in deep grass.

"They would have gone a lot farther," he told me
on the way back, his arm around my bony shoulder,
"if it wasn't for the wind. A lot farther." Father,
it was always hard for me to judge your words.
I didn't understand that failure is a kind of high fly
which never carries where it should have,
that, no matter what ball field you choose,
there's always a wind blowing in from center.

Instead, as we walked silently through the thick grass toward home,
I just stared at his black wing-tip shoes,
the caked dust that didn't wipe off.

THE BASEBALL LOVER

So far it's a no-hitter.
She's still on the couch, staring at *Dateline*,
he's in the corner, oiling his glove
with his tongue.

This is the tension of extra innings—
all day he's waited on deck,
counting the circles chalked
on his brain.

She claims he wears his yellow baseball cap
too much. Sometimes he even sleeps with it
on his face like an egg yolk,
while her breathing makes the sound of wind
through empty bleachers.
All night, dreams flow from the cap's brim:
> He's sliding toward the plate
> and the slide never stops—through the dugout,
> under the grandstand, across the sandlot,
> into the skin of his childhood,
> the seat of his pants burning
> like birth.

At the commercial, he switches on the Twins game.
Someone is trying to steal home—
his legs
are the wings
of anxious birds.
He will never
move in slow
motion, not
even in the
replay. Here
comes the pitch

here comes
the runner,
he slides
    next to her on the couch,
    begins whispering sweet baseball scores
    into her ear.

SUMMER OF 1963:
THE ORBIT OF THE WIFFLE BALL

It didn't matter that the wind
blew your high pop-ups back to home plate,
didn't matter that a hard line drive stopped
dead in thick grass.
You just kept swinging the bat, believing the ball
would fly farther than it ever did.
You stared at the Wiffle ball, a tiny moon with holes in it,
and thought about John Kennedy on his inauguration,
speaking into the holes of a microphone.

Each time you connected, you
clacked the ball toward your house,
toward windows it could not shatter.
You and your friends were just kids,
and you swore you'd stay that way
forever. You ran the bases each day
until you wore a dirt path in
your fathers' patience,
until your mothers swung open the screen door,
and you slid into home for dinner.

Unbreakable, the cardboard Wiffle ball box claimed.
But the white plastic cracked after two weeks of batting,
so you returned it to the Ben Franklin store for a new one.
Walking proudly on the buckled sidewalk, you turned
the new ball over and over, imagining you
held the whole world in the palm of your hand.

In August, you stood alone in your yard at dusk,
not realizing how cold the winds would be in November.
Your bat perched like a rifle on your shoulder,
you braced yourself as the breeze picked up, the national anthem
caught in your ear,
your pants wrapping and unwrapping around your ankles
like flags.

That summer all you could think about was
tomorrow, how high you could hit a Wiffle ball
when your arm muscles turned eighteen.
You'd send it flying all the way to the moon.
The future was out there
like a pop fly dropping from space,
and you'd be waiting for it—your small, growing hands
outstretched,
your faith unbreakable.

SURVIVING THE TERRORISM:
ODE TO A BASEBALL WOUND

Wound, you began as a blossom of pain
beneath the skin on that close play. When I rose from
the slide at third base, you rose
to the scarlet surface, innocent and blushing
on the skin of my calf.
At first, you were the sky over my childhood at dawn.

That night, while I slept, you
stayed up all night, wrapping the sheet around yourself,
staining the black night red.

I know you'll never heal if I keep you hidden.
I have to open you to
the sun, the rain, the sandpaper winds.

Wound, you're the shape of America
on my skin. You're the shape of suicide bombs,
of wars, of festering fear. You're the anguished shape
of something we wake to
when our dreams suddenly end.

As I limp, my friends shake their heads.
I'll carry you around
a long time; wounds are like that—
the fresh pink skin seals over them,
but they never really disappear.
Maybe I'll carry the faint scar to my death.
The undertaker, dressing me,
will shake his head at the leg
and mutter *I hope you were safe*.

AFTER THE TOKENS RUN OUT

On the advice of a marriage counselor, a couple stopped at a baseball batting cage "to work off some steam." The owner remarked that "They kept coming back for more and more tokens."

—Minneapolis Star Tribune

Standing in adjacent cages, husband and wife miss
and miss and miss,
can't get their timing down.
Between pitches, they
sigh at the crisscrossed metal sky.

They swing, grunting and swearing,
pulling the bat around through resistant air.
Beneath heavy red batting helmets, their faces fight gravity.
They glare at the machine that, once every six seconds,
hurls a ball toward them like a tiny hissing world.
Always out of reach, it thunks
into the tarp behind home plate.

After twelve swings they step out of the cages.
Still not speaking to each other,
they stand at the booth, flap dollars on the counter
for more tarnished tokens,
feed them into the slot that's always hungry.
Slower, they both think. *A little slower this time.*

After a few pitches they finally begin to connect:
    He leans into the pitches the way he did
    in the high school playoffs.
    Though the flight of the ball is cut
    off by the heavy net, he imagines it
    clearing the fence in deep center.
    She sees day after dull day spinning
    toward her like balled-up wash rags. One by one
    she surprises them
    with a slap in the face.

After the tokens run out, they meet again
between the two cages, pause there, notice the
redness in each other's cheeks.
They speak to each other in soft gasps,
the sweat trickling down their faces so easily
it could be tears.

THE EX-BASEBALL STAR STEPS OUT OF RETIREMENT

He cracks a few fly balls, the bat in his hands
remembering those long drives, homers
the crowd confused with
migrating white
birds.

The older you get, he thinks, the more you notice
the chalk lines, chalk lines
on the grass, on your face.

He lopes to the outfield. Trying to make
a perfect peg from center to second
is like aiming a frayed shoelace
through a rusted eyelet.

Dust wheezes in the hourglass of his throat
as he steps over the third base
line, into the empty dugout.

He'll shuffle home, rake the yard, sip a beer.
He'll watch his sons play catch by the fence,
the ball game blaring on the scratchy speakers of the radio.

PLAYING THE WIND: RUNNING FOR FLY BALLS IN EARLY SPRING

Those high fly balls in early spring
look so easy at first, then catch you off
balance when the wind
pushes them with its huge transparent fingers.
You love this game,
but there's always one
that can make a fool out of you
in front of everyone, catch you
turning the wrong
way, your glove raised in the air
as though it's waving goodbye.

Play the wind, someone once said.
Whoever said that wasn't standing on a flat field,
the whole sky trying to blow him out like a last candle.
The sun you hoped for slides behind an eye patch
of cloud, and all afternoon the ball plays tricks on you.
A chameleon, it takes on the color of its background:
rippling cirrus, a sheet blowing on a clothesline.
When the earth shifts beneath your dizzy feet
like the slanting floor of a Tilt-A-Whirl,
you realize you're just along for the ride.

Love is a little like that—you lean forward,
thinking you're ready,
but when your partner swings
in the distance, you're blind.
The ball climbs,
following a lost kite tail somewhere in the air,
and all you can do is turn your face upward
as though it could catch the rain you're sure is about to fall.

Convinced you can't judge the flight
of a baseball any more, you give up,
cross the field toward home. That's when it happens:
whatever it is that drops from the sky to your glove
fits there so naturally, as if it was always there,
right in the palm of your hand.

PITCHER WHOSE HEART WAS STOPPED BY A LINE DRIVE TO THE CHEST

All the years of throwing
have come to this:
    your best pitch flying back at you,
    startling the air at twice the speed.

Then there's the crack
the whole stadium must hear:
you gather the ball's impact into your chest,
a leather knot that won't untie.

Your life doesn't flash before you, like they say.
The present simply splinters

and you teeter, as if you're balancing
atop the upper deck roof, looking for
a long fly that will not come down.

As you fall toward home,

you're the kid in the sandlot
perfecting pitches until the ball turns
to a shaft of pure light.
It's the ninth, two outs.
You're releasing your fast one

and the batter

    connects, the ball climbing
    and climbing, hissing far above
    the fence, toward your house across the street,
    your bedroom window waiting to shatter.

AGING MAN, SEARCHING FOR THE LOST BASEBALL

He's crawled on hands and knees into deepest grass:
a thousand hiding places there,
a thousand small green stadiums.
His palm is a mine detector,
but round stones lie to him,
thistles scratch red chalk lines on his wrists.

Behind him, home plate
is blurred by dust or a swirl of gray
weeds. He pauses
like a newspaper caught in the brush.
In the headlines he sees all the games
he's lost. He's never hit a baseball
far enough to replace the moon.

A thousand boys like the one he once was
fill the bleachers that creak
like the sound of crickets
singing the national anthem.

Crouching empty-handed, he knows
how foolish it was to think
the red jersey of his heart
should be raised on the flagpole
for everyone to cheer.

TWISTERS

What else is there to do but
aim his pickup into this empty baseball field
and spin?
The concentric ruts
are the circles under his eyes.
Dust devils curl behind the truck—
he imagines them swirling
like cyclones down Main Street,
tearing the tin grain elevator apart,
bringing the water tower to its knees.

He curses the gray screen that formed
between him and his woman last night—
the way she would only talk
through a locked hollow-core door,
his lips feeling the wood vibrate.

He cranks the wheel until
his elbows ache, the losing pitcher
whose curveball's lost its break,
accelerates until his toes are blisters.

He believes dust will turn to gold,
believes he could spin and
spin, digging deeper into the land, spin
until he carves a shallow lake
in the center of this parched field, spin
the rest of his life,
but the engine
dies.

Climbing onto the hood,
he watches the last of the dust:
a small twister
the soft breeze tears apart
before it reaches the edge of town.

END OF THE SEASON:
THE TOUGH-LUCK BALLPLAYER IN
THE DIAMOND BLUFF TAVERN

His wounds are always on the inside, nothing
you can see. On a long throw from
center to home, he heard the glass marbles
in his elbow shattering.

It always happened years ago, in a high school playoff
or state championship game. In the bar,
sipping a slow beer, he'll tell you about the knee:
after a great stop at short or third,
he pivoted, felt the whole world beneath
him pop out of its socket.
He's never turned the same since, not even to look
into his wife's eyes.

He inhales his cigarette deep into his lungs.
Wisps of gray scale the outfield walls of his temples.
He'll tell you he'll be back in men's league
as soon as this one heals.
Beneath his skin, the old blood rushes to feed distant muscles.

No, the world doesn't go up in smoke all at once—
it falls apart little by little:
tendon, hamstring, ankle, wrist.
Those moments replay their bright pain over and over
in his dreams some nights.

He'll tell you it was last of the ninth, two outs,
the crowd on their feet.
His fingers whiten on an invisible baseball.
You know by the squint in his eyes
that he's seeing it happen again,
that his life depended on that play.
He drains the beer, eases the sweating bottle to the counter

as though sliding the handle of a bat
into the dugout rack, then
limps out of the bar, his
past a bandage taped gently,
gently around one knee.

THE OLD MEN OF SUMMER

1

Those foolish old ball players:

they take the field too early, patches of snow
still on the outfield grass. For blocks, you can hear
their muscles wheeze,
the rusty door hinges of junkyard cars.
Running the bases at full speed, they slip
on ice, their kneecaps shattering like lightbulbs.
The next day, you might see them in front of retirement homes
in wheelchairs. Dazed, they talk to the insides
of wrinkled ball caps: *I should of tried for an inside-the-parker,*
they keep muttering. *I should of.*

2

One lingers in the darkened batter's box in late August,
the night game over, the bleachers hollow, floodlights gone blind.
He crouches in his stance for one more at bat,
cleats digging their false teeth into the dirt.
He raises his aluminum bat high, stirring the tarpaulin
of gray clouds gathering overhead.
Tipping his head back, he calls out with the voice
of the cream-faced little leaguer
he used to be back in '38:
Come on pitcher. Gimmie your best shot. I dare you.
He braces himself, the wind rippling
his shirttail like a pennant.
When lightning fires its fast ball from the clouds
and strikes the bat,
his body glows like a filament.

Outside the ball park, small boys, fingers clasped in the
diamond fence, blink
as the whole empty field
lights up for a moment.

PART FOUR

Soul Highway

FIRST DAY OF SUMMER VACATION: MUSKRAT ON A SUBURBAN ROADSIDE

Struck by a car bumper, it prances around and
around in a circle on
the shoulder of the road,
its red wet face held high, pink
teeth bared as the rush-hour traffic
crawls past.

Someone could have stopped their car,
tried to coax the animal back to the woods.
Someone could have swerved, let
the anxious treads
stop his crazed dance.

The light turns green. I
accelerate like the rest of the cars.
In the rear-view mirror I can still see
the muskrat, tracing the same circle,
his tilted face looking beyond all metal and chrome
toward the sky, where the moon would rise tonight
above the shopping centers,

moon that would shine down on him
as he circles
the same way my car would be circling
in some motel parking lot,
my knuckles too bloodless on the wheel
for it to turn without my will.

I'd circle there for
hours, wasting my vacation,
my tires crushing the summer moonlight
that will coat the asphalt
like the lightest of snow.

THE ARROWHEAD

Back from his hike, all Dad gave me was a chipped stone, its edges
like a jagged mountain range, so I'd know
the soil I walked on was deep. All he gave me
were words I didn't understand: *Ojibwe, Hochunk, Wonkshiek.*
All he gave me was a stare, its point sharp enough to cut.
   I was a son who thought only of
    hanging out with my buddies by the river, the growl
    of mufflers, the colors of the girls' blouses in my class.
   I knew just a handful of years, not five or six hundred.
   I was a boy who lived in water, not in stone.
He showed me the chipped surface
with his pudgy fingers. *Like ripples,*
almost, he said, *like there's a current, or*
a wind blowing on its surface. He studied the stone
as though it could show him which direction to go.

Now his words are frozen in that flint.
I hand it to my son, this stone,
pointed enough to draw blood. Beneath
his fingers its surface must feel
like ripples, almost.

HUNTING FOR NIGHT CRAWLERS

1

We wrapped red cellophane around our flashlights
so light became a lie to them.
We tried not to let our bare feet
touch the earth as we stalked.

Their elastic bodies were silver,
stretched clean like our minds.
We lunged, grasped
them between thumb and forefinger,
then pulled slowly. We learned how much
a night crawler loves the center of the earth:
sometimes we'd lose the tug of war
and they'd snap
in two. Half worms oozed thickened mud
onto our palms.
If we pulled just right
they emerged: taut, thick bass strings,
music filling the whole yard.

2

They weren't like garter snakes.
Whenever we'd see one in the yard, we'd
run, screaming for the hoe.
Once Dad chopped one to pieces.
An hour later, I lifted the garbage can lid,
stared in terror at
small segments of yellow and black,
each one still writhing.

3

We lifted plywood lids to whole washtubs
of night crawlers, layered with coffee grounds and leaves.
All summer, for fifty cents a dozen, we reached deep
for fishermen, the soil itself coming alive in our open hands.

4

Some days, after a downpour,
night crawlers washed across our driveway.
Later, we'd find them floating in puddles:
too pale. Too pale.

5

Thirty years later, there are times when you and I
stop talking in the dark,
the dim bulbs of our eyes covered
with cellophane. We lose them, keep
losing them.

We know our skin's no longer elastic.
We stare out the bedroom window,
notice the dirt caked on the glass.

And sometimes, after a rain, we take a walk,
stepping on night crawlers on the sidewalk
without even seeing them.

MY FATHER AND THE DANCING BEARS

They stand on hind legs like the rest of us,
they ride bicycles around a paint-chipped ring.
The trainer pulls on their chains, cracks his whip, the sudden
snap startling the stale air of the big top.
My father sits beside me
in the grandstand, a half-smile tugging at his face.

A tiny red bellboy's cap slanting on its head,
one bear groans and bounces a ball on its nose—
its flabby sides shudder
and the crowd ripples with laughter.
The second bear, eyes dazed, tongue dangling
from the side of its mouth, dances in a too-tight, sequined blue tux.
The crowd exhales an amused *Ohhhh*, spills popcorn
between slats in the bleachers.
The bear doesn't realize its claws will never click against
the bark of a tree in the wilderness—
it's destined to dance this absurd, collared waltz
day after day, even though it could turn
and crush its trainer in an instant.

Today I keep seeing my father,
hunched, heavy on that bowed wooden bleacher,
unable to take his eyes off those bears.
It's his day off from work, from his string of traveling sales jobs
where he peddled clothes dryers, children's banks, grain—the bits of gold.
Like suits two sizes too small, the jobs never quite fit him.
His white salesman's shirt is clean,
but stained faintly beneath the arms.
He could have hugged me with those arms,
snapping a rib.

That afternoon there were dancing bears to watch, but for a moment,
I couldn't stop looking at my father,
his face suddenly boyish, transfixed by
the bear riding a bicycle around and
around the scuffed wooden ring.

Because he didn't say, I'll never know what he was thinking.
Maybe he was wondering:
How do you train an 800-pound bear to balance like that?
How can it stand upright on its hind legs for so long?
Or maybe he was just entranced by the bear for being what it was—
 a wild animal, tamed by this strange world
 of striped canvas and sawdust and cages.
 A huge beast, pedaling a bike too small for it,
 circling in a delicate waltz,
 doing whatever it was asked,
 making us almost smile for a few seconds.

THE DANCE OF THE RIPPLES

The Saturday evening after Dad's funeral we find ourselves at the lake,
and Mom wades alone into the calm, darkening water.
Deep in grief, her skin is the color of silt. Concentric circles
move out from her thighs. The small ripples
hurry away from her, travel the distance
to the shore and reach us, her children,
who stand still, ankle-deep, unable to talk, the humid blanket
of dusk weighting down our shoulders.

At this lake tonight, everything
seems too quiet or too loud, rising or falling, moving or not moving.
One of us exhales with a soft hiss.

We watch her wade into deeper water, up to her waist, though
we all know she doesn't swim.
But it's her heart we worry about now, her small
red heart drowning inside the twilight of her body.
I want to call out to her:
Not so deep, not so deep. He's not here
to steady you when you step
into the drop-off.

Suddenly, music wafts through the screen of the pavilion:
Glenn Miller's saxophones roll smoothly toward us.
Mother faces the center of the lake.
Forgetting for a moment, she sways side to side to the rhythm,
sending out small sudden waves that glisten in the moonlight.
It seems as though someone should ask her to dance.
Then she closes her eyes, silencing the music
while the ripples clasp their rings
tightly around her waist,
holding her, holding her.

FINDING A NOTE TO MYSELF:
THROW AWAY THOSE OLD SHOES

After fifteen years, they're still curled in my closet,
dreaming of sidewalks and distance.

Nothing could make these worn shoes new again:
not creamy brown polish to erase the maps in their leather skin,
not thread to seal their smiling torn seams,
not walking backwards across the whole country.

These shoes feel no more pain—
all the squeaks are softened out of them.
They know their way home so well
they could stride down the street without me.

How my wife has hated these shoes. They smell
too much like pungent sweat, too much like
all the wrong roads I've taken. *Throw them,* she said,
do them a favor and throw them away.
How many times, in the darkness after spring cleanings,
have I crept out to the garbage can in my socks
to retrieve them?

When I slip them on again this morning,
They cling to my feet, desperate as old lovers.
I can feel the holes in the bottoms—
leather-rimmed eyes that stare
up through my feet

into the telescopes of my legs
at all the miles I'll walk the next fifteen years.

THE SYMMETRY OF BRUISES

Bruise in the middle of my palm—
like a dark storm cloud to some,
but to me: good. A promise of needed rain, a blue rising
where, as I leaped for it, the baseball struck leather and
stopped. Bruise on my
palm: the mouth of a purple cave opening. In my sleep
it's a portal to those who have come before me—
spirits of the old ballplayers, my father, my grandfather—
who once popped fists in their mitts
and now lie watching me from beneath the level grass.
Save my memory, they say, and I do, little by little,
as I snag each line drive,
tendons stretching to the sky.

Bruise on my palm: growing even larger,
expanding through tender flesh and capillaries
like a thunderhead reaching across my hometown,
covering its stockyards, its railroad cars
with aching wheels, its cracked highways
tied in concrete knots, its parched cornfields
waiting for the ozone smell of rain.
Bruise reaching over my whole childhood,
shadowing a backyard, sealing over my initials carved in a tree,
the swaybacked roof of the house where I was born,
comforting me, my oxygen-starved face crying as I
gasped for air for the first time,
the same way I would gasp, years later, when I made that catch
on a sandlot, my palm burning beautifully with bee stings,
my past and future, the whole world,
nothing but blue,
blue, blue.

MY FATHER'S CLOSET

Crawling in on hands and knees,
I'm the darkest corner of this closet,
my thumb hooked in the noose

of a red and blue necktie. A pale frayed salesman's shirt
floats above me, a ghost
searching for someone

to haunt. I've showered off the scent of my father—
traces of sweat and failure
that had begun to slick down my hair,
cling to my body, a second skin.
I walked to this closet clean and ready,
my receding forehead washed of

all its wrinkled roads. Now I'm wandering among
fallen trousers—dim pools of tweed and wool and herringbone.
Above me, rows of suit jackets steal my
oxygen. A leather suitcase still carries
the odors of blackened diner grills, Lucky cigarettes,
hotel lobbies with stained carpets, the warmed
plastic of telephone receivers. I imagine a voice

sliding through them:
Can I interest you in a new Maytag?
I'm not sure if it's my voice or his.
That's when I feel it, and I can't move:
the fear of not finding my way out

suddenly covers me,
a landslide of worn-out shoes.

ANOTHER STORY OF THE OLIVES

How much did their blind eyes see?
Symmetrically placed in a gallon jar, the red pimentos
facing outward, the olives stared at our town
from the tall front window of The Hub Café.

For years the eyes kept watch on the square each Friday night:
the junior high punks slipping into narrow shadows to battle or kiss;
the blue exhaust from teens' cars lurching past, needles stabbing at empty,
wrong way on a one-way street;
the old ones on park benches, crumpling into newspapers
that tumble and scrape across the intersection at 2 a.m.
For years they saw the wars come and go, the flag
on the city hall pole rising and billowing and falling still.

I hated the way they watched me walk past in grade school,
scuffing the concrete with my Hush Puppies.
I hated the way they stared, as if waiting
for me to do something.

What boredom or madness drove old Mr. Hubb, years ago
in the back room of the café, to submerge them, one by
one, in this jar of liquid?
Maybe the kids around town were growing wild, so
someone needed to arrange
a thousand green olives
into a small, perfect life, shoulder to shoulder, not a space between.

If you looked closely, their spirals seemed to march in circles
as if they were traveling all the way around the world,
then back to this one-gallon jar,
its tarnished tin cap
crimped so tightly
no one could
ever open
it.

A CERTAIN LENGTH OF LINE

When my son casts the lure, it arcs high above the water,
skimming the blue sky without hooking it.
It's a motion his gruff-voiced grandfather taught him:
this casting, this keeping time with the pendulum of a fishing pole.
It's a lure grandpa gave him a year before he died.
My son knows the old Hula Popper lure isn't perfect:
its plug-shape covered with chipped red and yellow enamel,
uneven black spots on its back
as though painted by some trembling hand.
But he casts and casts anyway, hoping the lake will dream a fish
to bite on it. He waits, certain the lure will catch something
bigger than he ever imagined.

He lets the lure float on the calm surface a few seconds,
then dances it left, right—he's a conductor,
swinging his baton, the orchestra following with quick
crescendo notes.
             The dance stops abruptly.
The lure's two black eyeballs are caught in surprise
as a huge bass closes
the night sky on it.

He sets the hook deep, leaning as far back as he can
into the sunset. The largemouth bass leaps high
into the air, splashes,
the tiny tidal waves carrying
to the far shore. Then something

snaps. He stares in disbelief:
the line he thought could reel in the moon
dangles in front of him, fragile as a spider web threaded
between two clotheslines.

Back in the cabin, he sulks, whispers to the big picture window,
blind with the evening's darkness:
Grandpa's lure, lost. Lost.
The next day he whispers the word to the snapped cattails
and hollow trees, to the frogs that pull the swamp
over their heads, to the bird's nest, its powder blue eggshells
shattered on hard ground.

The following spring,
something floats to the surface along our shore,
its wide eyes rising between the green clouds of lily pads.
        He lifts it from the water,
gazes at the red and yellow lure
rotating in the sun, the ripples of morning air gliding out from it.

He finds the end of the short length of transparent line,
squeezes it tightly in his palm
as though he'll never let it go, as though he can feel someone pulling
gently, but insistently, on the other end.

FRICTION

You tell me you would get in a car and drive,
just drive until the blue dome of sky finally heats up
and all these snowdrifts melt, until the bare lips of mud
dream of grass. And I tell you
I am that car,
that I'm carrying you down the highway
as fast as I can,
my tires wobbling, my radiator bleeding,
green drops splattering on the concrete.

This was supposed to be easy, this quick press
on the accelerator that takes us all the way
to the edge of a dream, the place where
rocky earth crumbles, where
water massages the land like a hand caressing flesh,
like my hand caressing your flesh.

But friction always catches up with us—
tires sag, and metal against metal has no choice
but to wear down, until we're nothing more than
axles and pistons gone bad,
like the dark bones of cars we passed
stacked in salvage yards.
I want to say *Life is a radiator with fresh antifreeze,*
but this isn't funny. Life's more like a U-joint that's worn,
bearings that clash together on tight curves.
It's ice in the gas line, an oil light
glaring red with no station in sight.

I want to tell you *I'm your car,* but I'm more like
the wheezing wheels spinning.
No, I'm more like the dust rising behind us
as you gaze into the rearview mirror.

Still, we drive and drive all day and so what
if we can't see out the windshield plastered
with frost, so what if the engine skips
a few heartbeats and shudders,
so what? At sunset I pull over, let the car idle
and touch your shoulder.
There is no wearing down between
fingertips and skin, there is no corrosion.
We stare into each other's eyes.
Rust is a kind of fire, after all, I want to tell you.
Our eyes are a kind of fire, after all.

BILL MEISSNER

is the author of three books of poetry and a collection of short
stories. His writing has appeared in more than 150 journals,
magazines, and anthologies. His numerous awards include a
National Endowment for the Arts Creative Writing Fellowship,
five PEN/NEA Syndicated Fiction Awards, two Loft-McKnight
Awards, and a Minnesota State Arts Board Fellowship.
Meissner is the Director of Creative Writing at St. Cloud
State University in St. Cloud, Minnesota.